Girls' NIGHT IN

Gemma Barder

QEB

Editor: Tasha Percy
Designer: Rosie Levine
Editorial Director: Victoria Garrard
Art Director: Laura Roberts-Jensen
Girl Illustrations: Katy Jackson
Steps Illustrations: Jessica Secheret
Photography: Michael Wicks
Cakes supplied by Rosa Citrano - Rosa's Cakes
Crafts made by Caroline Stamps - Sew Happy

First published in the US in 2016 by
QEB Publishing
Part of The Quarto Group
6 Orchard
Lake Forest, CA 92630

A catalogue record for this book is available from the Library of Congress.

ISBN: 978 1 60992 955 8

Printed in China

Website information is correct at time of going to press. However, the publishers cannot accept liability for any information or links found on third-party websites.

Picture credits (t=top, b=bottom, l=left, r=right, c=center, FC=front cover, BC=back cover)

Shutterstock: FC tl Andrew Burgess, FC tl Byjeng, FC tl Butterfly Hunter, FC tcl Media Guru, FC tcr Alexandra Lande, FC c Mike Degteariov, FC cr Lipik, FC clb Sasimoto, BC tl Byjeng, BC tcl Lipik, BC tc Butterfly Hunter, BC tcr kanate, BC cl nemlaza, BC c Mike Degteariov, BC cr lyeyee, BC cb Picsfive, BC br lalan, BC bc Richard Peterson BC bcr NuDesign.co, 1, 3 Dovile Kuusiene, 4tl Lipik, 4tr Byjeng, 4cr lyeyee, 4ca, 5bl Mike Degteariov, 8tl Byjeng, 8cl Maaike Boot, 9tr nikkytok, 9c Andrew Burgess, 9bl Sergiy Telesh, 10tl, tr Media Guru, 10tc, c leosapiens, 10b Danny Smythe, 11tr, 12tl, tr, cl, br leosapiens, 12tc, c, bc Dinga, 12cra Africa Studio, 12bl Doungtawan, 13tl Richard Peterson, 13tr, cla Dinga, 13c tuulijumala, 13b vectorlib.com, 14tr Coffee-mill, 14c VadiCo, 14cr Aaron Amat, 14bl Shawn Hempel, 15br natashamam, 16tl Stephen Rees, 16tl Lipik, 16clb tomer turjeman, 16bl Morozova Oxana, 16bl Kitch Bain, 17tr lynea, 17cl leosapiens, 17cl Media Guru, 17crb Olga Popova, 17br Stephen Rees, 17bl lyeyee, 18tr lynea, 18b MNI, 19tr leosapiens, 20tr Mrsiraphol, 20cra MarijaPili-ponyte, 20cl, br Sasimoto, 20cr April70, 20bl Sarah2, 21tr, cr Byjeng, 22cr Kim Nguyen, 22bl Tatiana Volgutova, 22br Elena Kazanskaya, 23tc Nattika, 23tr Sailorr, 23cr Ian 2010, 23br Evgeny Karandaev, 24tl Maaike Boot, 24tc Alexandra Lande, 24tr Africa Studio, 25tc, c Sasimoto, 26tr, c, cra, cb, br Byjeng, 26cr Sasimoto, 26crb pzAxe, 26bl Aroonsak, 27cr gresei, 27bc, 28t Africa Studio, 28cr daffodilred, 28crb cvm, 28cb, 29tr homydesign, 29cr daffodilred, 29crb Lipskiy, 29br pukach, 30tr daffodilred, 30tr Tatiana Volgutova, 32tr Kim Nguyen, 32bl aboikis, 34-35 background Valentyn Volkov, 35br Lipik, 37c R-studio, 38tl Kamenuka, 38cl Igor Shikov, 39t, tl Kamenuka, 39tl Michael Kraus, 39cr Tanya K, 40tr nemlaza, 40cl, 41tr Real Illusion, 42bl nemlaza, 46tr bobyramone, 46tr Shelby Allison, 48tr kanate, 48c Evgeny Karandaev, 48cr Tarasyuk Igor, 48cl Maks Narodenko, 48cl Dionisvera, 48br razihusin, 50tr Ilya Akinshin, 51tr Andrew Burgess, 51tr R-studio, 51br Feng Yu, 52 Little_Desire, 53br Ilaszlo, 54bl jeehyun, 54bc mayakova, 54br Kawia Scharle, 55tr casejustin, 55 Mshev, 56tr, cr, br lalan, 56br Mike Degteariov, 58c paulina8, 58br sagir, 58br Julia Zakharova, 59cr Karkas, 60tr, tl, br Martina Vaculikova, 60tc, cl, cb, 61tl Studio_G, 61tc,c Martina Vaculikova, 62tl, tr grzhmelek, 62cra, c Maaike Boot, 62br Marine's, 63tl grzhmelek, 63b Vitaly Korovin, 64-65t zzveillust, 66l AlenKadr, 66bl Xenium, 66cl Picsfive, 66br Byjeng, 66tr Butterfly Hunter, 68tr optimarc, 68bl Richard Peterson, 68bl Evgeny Karandaev, 68br, 69tr Byjeng, 69tr Andrew Burgess, 69crb Dja65, 69br nikkytok, 69bc Bennyartist, 69bl Karina Bakalyan, 70tl Mike Degteariov, 70cr Coprid, 71tl, cra, bl Xenium, 71tr, cr, bc Bennyartist, 72tl Xenium, 72tr Bennyartist, 72cl Byjeng, 72bc Nancy Bauer, 72br Byjeng, 72cr Mike Degteariov, 73tl, tc, bl Byjeng, 73tr Bennyartist, 73cra MNI, 73ca, c Mike Degteariov, 76-77t, 76tr, br NuDesign.co, 78tr, cr, br Picsfive, 78br AlenKadr, 79cr Picsfive, 81bl, br NuDesign.co, 81cra AlenKadr, 81crb, 82tr MNI, 82tr Mike Degteariov, 84tr casejustin, 89tr, 92tl, tr, cl ekler, 92bl Lightspring, 93 Dan Kosmayer, 94tr PILart, 94br pics4sale, 95tr nemlaza, 95cr Lightspring, 95cr Media Guru, 95bl ekler

When you see this symbol ask for an adult's help.

Contents

Meet the Girls...

The secret to having the best girls'
night in is...the girls themselves!
Meet **Tommako**, **Jessie**, **Tye**, and **Sofia**.
Just like most friends, they each have their
own style and different things they like to
do, but they all have one thing in common—
they LOVE having a girly night in.

♥ NAME:
Tommako

Eye color:
Dark brown

♥ Hair color: Black
♥ Star sign: Leo
♥ Favorite color: Black, purple, and red
♥ Favorite animal: Dolphin
♥ Favorite music: Rock!
♥ Favorite subject: Music
♥ Favorite food: Thai green curry
♥ Hobbies: learning guitar, sketching, and
browsing thrift store for vintage finds.

♥ NAME:
Jessie

Eye color:
Blue

♥ Hair color: Blonde
♥ Star sign: Aquarius
♥ Favorite color: Pink
♥ Favorite animal: My dog Gatsby
♥ Favorite music: Pop
♥ Favorite subject: Creative writing
♥ Favorite food: Shrimp linguine
♥ Hobbies: Writing, baking, and
spending time with my friends.

♥ NAME:
Tye

Eye color:
Hazel

♡ Hair color: Brown
♡ Star sign: Gemini
♡ Favorite color: Turquoise
♡ Favorite animal: Cat
♡ Favorite music: Songs I can dance to
♡ Favorite subject: Art and design
♡ Favorite food: Sushi
♡ Hobbies: Shopping, styling my girls, and giving them makeovers.

♥ NAME:
Sofia

Eye color:
Brown

♡ Hair color: Light brown
♡ Star sign: Pisces
♡ Favorite color: Yellow
♡ Favorite animal: Tiger
♡ Favorite music: Anything upbeat
♡ Favorite subject: Sports and photography
♡ Favorite food: Grilled chicken salad
♡ Hobbies: When I'm not training, I love going to the movies or having a DVD night.

All about this book!

This book is pretty special, check out what it's all about.

Top Tip
If you don't want to theme your night in, just take ideas from each section.

★ This book is divided into lots of cool sections. Each section talks about a different theme such as **crafting**, **sleepovers**, **music**, or **games**.

★ Each section is hosted by one of the girls—they love talking about their favorite things!

★ At the *beginning* of each section there is a fun **quiz** to complete, plus cool invitations to make.

★ By the end of each section, you'll be an expert on how to host the perfect **girls' night in**.

Star Signs

Discover which star sign you are, then find out what it says about you. You can even find out which other star signs make your perfect friendship match!

Aquarius

January 20th—February 18th

The Water-bearer

You love making friends and inviting them over for a girls' night in. Although you're happiest when you've found that one perfect friend.

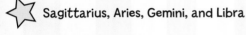 Sagittarius, Aries, Gemini, and Libra

Pisces

February 19th—March 20th

The Fish

You are a caring friend, and all your friends turn to you for a hug and a talk. You love being creative, and can always be trusted with a secret.

Capricorn, Taurus, Cancer, and Scorpio

Aries

March 21st—April 19th

The Ram

As an Aries, you enjoy being in charge. If there are plans to be made, you love making them. You also like helping your friends, from difficult homework to fashion decisions.

Gemini, Aquarius, Leo, and Sagittarius

Taurus

April 20th—May 20th

The Bull

You are uber-organized. In fact, I bet you can't remember the last time you forgot something you needed for school. Friends love having you around because you take the time to listen to them.

 Pisces, Cancer, Virgo, and Capricorn

Gemini

May 21st—June 20th

The Twins

Friends are really important to you, and it's a good thing, too, because you are great at making them. You're a real chatterbox, but you're great at listening, too.

Aries, Leo, Libra, and Aquarius

Cancer

June 21st—July 22nd

The Crab

Even though you might be the quietest girl in your group, you make an amazing friend. You're really loyal and will never forget a friend's birthday. You love hanging out with your family, too.

 Taurus, Virgo, Scorpio, and Pisces

= Star sign buddies

Leo

July 23rd—August 22nd

The Lion

You're really ambitious and can see yourself being famous one day (or the President—whichever comes first!). You enjoy being with people who like having fun.

 Gemini, Libra, Aries, and Sagittarius

Libra

September 23rd—October 22nd

The Scales

As a Libra, you're probably really sporty. But as you hate to be alone, you'll like being part of a team. You're great at talking to people and making new friends.

Leo, Sagittarius, Gemini, and Aquarius

Sagittarius

November 22nd—December 21st

The Archer

If there's fun to be had, you'll be the one to sniff it out. You always make time for things like homework because you want to spend as much time as possible with your friends.

Libra, Aquarius, Aries, and Leo

Virgo

August 23rd—September 22nd

The Maiden

You're a little shy and like to stay out of the spotlight. You really shine when there is a problem to be tackled, which is why all your friends ask you for advice.

Cancer, Scorpio, Taurus, and Capricorn

Scorpio

October 23rd—November 21st

The Scorpian

Scorpios are strong-willed, but that's just because you're so passionate. Your friends love how much energy you have, and can't wait to spend time with you.

 Virgo, Capricorn, Cancer, and Pisces

Capricorn

December 22nd—January 19th

The Goat

You've probably had the same best friend forever. You are super loyal and prefer hanging out with the friends you've known for ages, rather than make new ones.

Scorpio, Pisces, Taurus, and Virgo

Friend Characteristics

If all your friends were exactly like you, it would be boring, right?
Find out what makes your friends (and you!) so much fun to be around.

Extrovert or Introvert?

We can all be a little bit introverted or extroverted sometimes—even if we don't realize it. Read the descriptions below and see which ones sound more like you. Then think about your friends—which one are they most like?

Extrovert

Loves making new friends

Can't wait for drama class!

Chatterbox

Always trying something new

Dreams of traveling the world

Introvert

Loves chilling out with friends and on her own

Great listener

Thoughtful

Thinks things through

Tye is a real chatterbox and can talk to anyone; she's a total extrovert.

Sofia loves trying new things but she's shy, too.

Tommako dreams of touring the world with her band, but she'd plan it all out.

Jessie likes to think about things and is quieter around people she doesn't know, which makes her more of an introvert. The thing is, you can be a mix of both.

Everyone is unique—that's what makes having different friends so much fun!

Friendship Portrait

Create a portrait of your friend or friend group using words and pictures.

1 Draw a picture of your friend, or your group of friends, on a piece of paper.

2 Take a piece of white cardstock (which is bigger than your drawing) and cut a square or circle out of the middle to frame your picture. Glue your picture behind your frame.

3 Decorate your frame; you could add hearts or stars or other fun designs. Think of all the wonderful words that come to mind when you think about your friend or friends, and write them around your frame.

When you have finished, glue a length of ribbon or string at the top of your frame so your friend can hang it on her wall.

YOU WILL NEED:

- Paper
- White cardstock
- Colored pens
- Paper glue
- Scissors
- String or ribbon

TYE

Cute · Funky · Loyal · Playful · Arty · Cool · Fun · Chatty · Sweet · Kind · Happy · Stylish

It's Movie Night!

Chilling out with your all-time favorite movies is one of the best ways to spend a night in. Check out my top tips!

Copy or trace this invite, then make more to hand out to your friends to let them know all the info on your perfect movie night in.

.... **is invited to**

MY MOVIE MARATHON NIGHT

Screenings will take place at

....

Starting at

....

Homemade popcorn will be served!

RSVP:

I'd love to come
or
Boo! I can't make it

The movie
I will bring is:

....

What's Your Movie Star Style?

Ever wondered what your perfect leading role would be? Take the quiz to find out!

YES

NO

 **START**

Love sports?

Know the lastest gossip?

Great at solving problems?

Kind of a daydreamer?

Always look your best?

Always get the giggles?

Kind of a daredevil?

Can you cry on demand?

Joker of the pack?

Up for an adventure?

Romantic Lead

You love a little drama in your life and even after you've been crying for eight hours straight, your hair and outfit always remain perfect. You would be great in a romance.

Comedy Star

You don't take life too seriously and you love making your friends giggle. You'd be great starring in a movie that gets the audience chuckling, even if you ended up looking silly in the process.

Super Sleuth

You love helping your friends solve their problems and you can't resist a good mystery. You aren't afraid to ask questions and love making people happy, too.

Action Hero

If you've slowed down long enough to read this quiz, you'll have discovered that you are perfect for an action role. Step aside Spider-man, there's a new hero in town!

The Screening Room

Enjoy your movies in style with these awesome ideas.

Take a Seat

Once you've decided where you're going to host your movie marathon, make sure you provide some super comfy seats for everyone. Arrange cushions, beanbags, pillows, and blankets in spots where everyone can see the screen.

Lights, Camera, Action!

Switch your main light off, but keep a few little lights on for friends who might need to find the bathroom halfway through your movie. String lights look really magical and give your room a cozy glow.

> Why not make a "Keep Quiet: Movie Watching in Progress!" sign for your screening room door?

Sshhh!

Just like at the real theater, unwanted noise can be a total pain. Make a "phones on silent" rule and let the rest of your family know your screening room is off limits.

Refreshments Available

There's nothing better than sipping your favorite drink or eating some delicious snacks during your movie. Check out page 14 for how to make your own yummy popcorn.

Movie Marathon Planner

Keep your movie night in full swing by knowing exactly what you're going to watch.

SCREENING SCHEDULE

Refreshments (grab a drink and some popcorn)

Take your seats (find your ideal spot)

MOVIE ONE

Refreshment break (and bathroom break!)

MOVIE TWO

Change into PJs and get some extra blankets

More snacks and drinks

MOVIE THREE

TOP TIPS
★★★★★

Start early! The last thing you want is to fall asleep before it's your turn to choose a movie.

42721672 1671 42721671 42721672

Think of your guests—don't show a scary movie if someone really doesn't want to be spooked.

Make sure everyone is comfy.

42721672 42721671 42721672 21671

Be a good hostess. Check that everyone has a drink and something to munch before the movie starts.

231769 231 231769

Pop-Tastic

Making popcorn is fun and easy to do, and you can add some yummy flavors to it, too! All you need are popcorn kernels, vegetable oil, and a saucepan.

1

Add some vegetable oil to a cold pan. About two tablespoons is good, or enough to cover the bottom of your pan.

2

Pour in enough popcorn kernels to cover the bottom of your pan, but don't overfill, or your popcorn won't pop.

3

Put the lid on your pan, turn it to a medium heat, and wait for the popping. Keep checking your popcorn and moving it around— you don't want it to burn.

Add sugar...

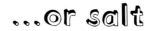

...or salt

4 Once all your kernels have popped, carefully spoon them out of the pan and into a bowl. Leave to cool for a couple of minutes— then it's time to add some flavor. Sprinkle sugar or drizzle honey for a sweet treat, or shake on some salt to go savory.

I like to add cinnamon to mine. YUM!

Movie Star Punch

Mix up this thirst quencher—it's perfect to enjoy while you watch your movies and munch your popcorn.

1

In a large jug, mix together your lemonade and orange juice. You want to have about one part orange juice to three parts lemonade.

Add more strawberries, lemon slices, and mint leaves for decoration.

2

Put most of your strawberries in a bowl and gently squish them with the back of a fork (you don't want to mash them completely).

3 For each glass, start with a teaspoon of strawberries at the bottom. Now pour over your fruit punch and pop in some mint leaves, a lemon slice, and a straw. So refreshing and glam, too!

15

Write Your Own Movie

Ever wished you and your friends could star in your very own movie? Don't just dream about it, make it happen!

When you've finished watching your favorite movies, get together to write your own movie using this guide.

Location, Location, Location

Think about where you want your movie to be set. If it's a story of friends and family, you could probably film it in your house or around where you live. If you're thinking of being more adventurous, you could turn your bedroom into a movie set. Cover it with sheets to make the surface of an alien planet, or set up tables and chairs to look like a restaurant.

Costume Drama

One of the best ways actors get into character is by putting on a costume. When you have your characters developed think about what they might wear, even if you're just borrowing your mom's night gown or your dad's hat!

The Stars of the Show

When you've written your movie, the next step is to cast it. Ask your friends which characters they would like to be. If two friends want to be the same character, put their names on separate pieces of paper, fold them up, and pick one out randomly.

The Crew

Not everyone will want to be in front of the camera, so think of jobs for your shyer friends to do. Someone needs to operate the camera, sort out props and costumes, and direct (that basically means bossing everyone around!).

The Script

Write out a couple of scenes from your movie for your friends to act out—or ask a creative friend to do it for you. You could make one of the scenes action-packed, and another slow and dramatic. The words might change as you start acting, but that's OK.

Prop It Up

Anything an actor uses in a performance is a prop— from a book to a bag of candy. Read your script and make a list of everything you need—then go on a hunt around your house to find them all. Ask your parents or siblings if you want to borrow anything.

Movie Spinner

Make this fun movie spinner game to help you decide which blockbuster you're going to watch next.

YOU WILL NEED:

- Pens or pencils
- Thin cardstock
- Paper glue
- Scissors
- Cotter pin

1 Draw a large circle on some thin cardstock. Divide it into eight sections and number them.

2 Add some color to the sections, then cut out the circle. Punch a small hole in the middle.

3 Draw an arrow on some cardstock (it should be smaller than the circle), and cut it out. Then punch a small hole in the middle.

4 Place the arrow on top of the circle—make sure the two holes line up.

5 Carefully push your cotter pin through the two holes, and then open it up at the back to secure it in place. Your arrow should now spin around.

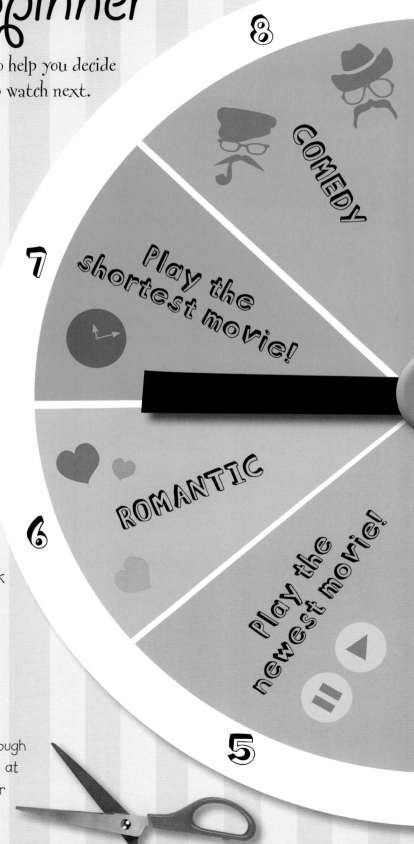

How to Play...

The circle contains the following spaces:

- 1 — Play the oldest movie!
- FANTASY
- 2
- Play the longest movie!
- 3
- SCARY
- 4

1

Pick movies that you want to watch and that match the eight spaces on the circle.

2

Each person takes a turn spinning the arrow, but on your first turn just look at the numbers.

3

Whoever spins the highest number gets to spin the arrow again and choose a movie.

Didn't get to pick a movie? That's a great excuse to plan another movie night.

Super Sleepover

Grab those sleeping bags and face masks, girls, we're going to have fun all night long...Well, at least until we all fall asleep!

You could use the template below to create some gorgeous invitations for your friends. Make sure you let them know just what they need to bring for the ultimate cozy sleepover.

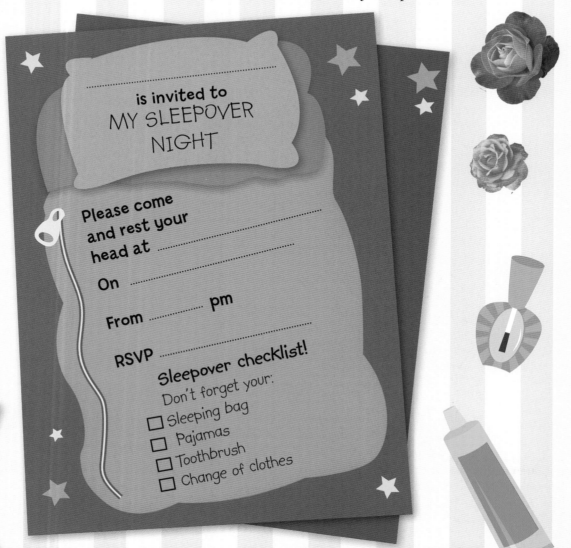

....

is invited to
MY SLEEPOVER
NIGHT

Please come and rest your head at ....

On ....

From .... **pm**

RSVP ....

Sleepover checklist!
Don't forget your:
☐ Sleeping bag
☐ Pajamas
☐ Toothbrush
☐ Change of clothes

Find Your New Look

One of the best things to do on a sleepover is to try out a whole new look. Answer the questions below to discover which look you should go for.

1 It's time to get ready for the school dance. What's on your mind?
- **a.** I want to look nice but I want to stand out, too.
- **b.** I'm going to dance all night so I need to feel comfortable.
- **c.** I need a whole new outfit.
- **d.** I wonder if there's going to be a band.

2 Which shopping venue makes you most excited?
- **a.** A vintage store.
- **b.** Online shopping is the way to go.
- **c.** The mall.
- **d.** Quirky, independent shops.

3 What do you LOVE about your wardrobe?
- **a.** It has some cool tops and dresses.
- **b.** It's so organized.
- **c.** There's so much space to fill with clothes.
- **d.** All the different styles.

4 What DON'T you love about your wardrobe?
- **a.** There isn't enough to make me stand out from the crowd.
- **b.** Those uncomfortable shoes I NEVER wear.
- **c.** The fact I don't have that top I saw in a magazine last week.
- **d.** It's a little messy...

5 Which time period do you like most?
- **a.** 1920s-1960s.
- **b.** Can I say the future?
- **c.** Right now!
- **d.** 1980s-1990s.

6 If you could go to any event, what would it be?
- **a.** A movie premieré.
- **b.** The Olympics.
- **c.** A fashion show.
- **d.** A music festival.

Mostly "a"s - Retro Girl
If you want to stand out from the crowd, but still look effortlessly cool—try the retro look. You can choose from lots of different styles—go 20s with fringed dresses or try bold black and white prints like the 60s.

Mostly "b"s - Laid-Back Cool
Turning down the dial on your look doesn't have to be dull. You can still look totally chic and keep up the comfort factor. Try over-sized tops with jeans and comfy boots. Scoop your hair into a messy ponytail, or wear it loose.

Mostly "c"s - Super Slick
Just like Tye, you love fashion, so a super-fashionable look is just for you. But you don't have to be super-rich to get the look. Choose an outfit you like from a magazine and try to recreate it with the clothes you already have.

Mostly "d"s - Rock Chick
For you, your look reflects who you are— a rock chick. If you care to try something a little different why not wear big boots with pretty dresses. A biker jacket and headphones help complete the look.

Pamper Time

Feeling totally pampered is an essential part of any slumber party. Get these ingredients ready before your guests arrive, then make them feel totally spoiled.

Luscious Locks

YOU WILL NEED:

- One banana
- One teaspoon of honey
- Bowl
- Fork
- Shower cap

Mash your banana until it is really smooth—if you have a blender, pop it in there and give it a whizz.

Add honey to the mashed banana and mix together.

How to Apply

Now comes the messy part! Starting at your roots (the hair closest to your head) start applying the mix. Use your fingers to spread it through your hair so that each section has some of the mixture on it.

Put a shower cap on and leave for **15-20 minutes.** Wash off and condition as you usually do. Not only will your hair feel great, it will smell pretty delicious, too!

Fabulous Face Mask

1

Carefully cut your avocado in half, take out the stone, then spoon the insides into a bowl.

YOU WILL NEED:

- One ripe avocado
- One tablespoon of honey
- Half a lemon
- Knife
- Spoon
- Bowl

2

Mash the avocado with the back of your spoon or a potato masher until it forms a paste. Now add the honey.

3

Finally, add a squeeze of lemon and give your mask mixture a good stir.

How to Apply

Fingers are best. Scoop up a good dollop of the mixture with your first and middle fingers, then gently rub it into your skin using circular motions. Cover your cheeks, nose, chin, and forehead.

Be VERY careful not to get any of the mixture in your eyes. After a few minutes, wipe off the mixture with a washcloth and splash your face with warm water.

Nailed It

You don't have to have perfect nails to try out this fun style. Check out my gorgeous twist on a classic French manicure.

YOU WILL NEED:

- Nail polish in two colors
- Nail polish remover
- Cotton balls

1

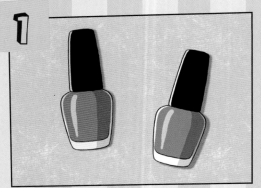

Choose two nail polishes to complement your style. You could go for a classic look, or something more adventurous.

2

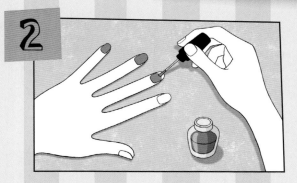

Paint all your nails using the *base color* (that's the color for the larger part of your nail). Make sure you paint from the *base* (or bottom) of your nail to the tip.

3

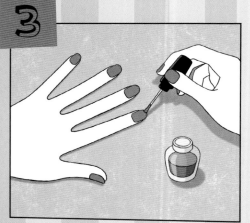

After your base color has dried, it's time to add the tips. Paint a sweep of polish over the top of your nail where the white tip would be. This can be a little tricky, so don't worry if you have to start again.

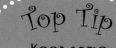

NAIL POLISH REMOVER

Top Tip

Keep some cotton balls and nail polish remover close by for cleaning up any polish that goes over the edge of your nails.

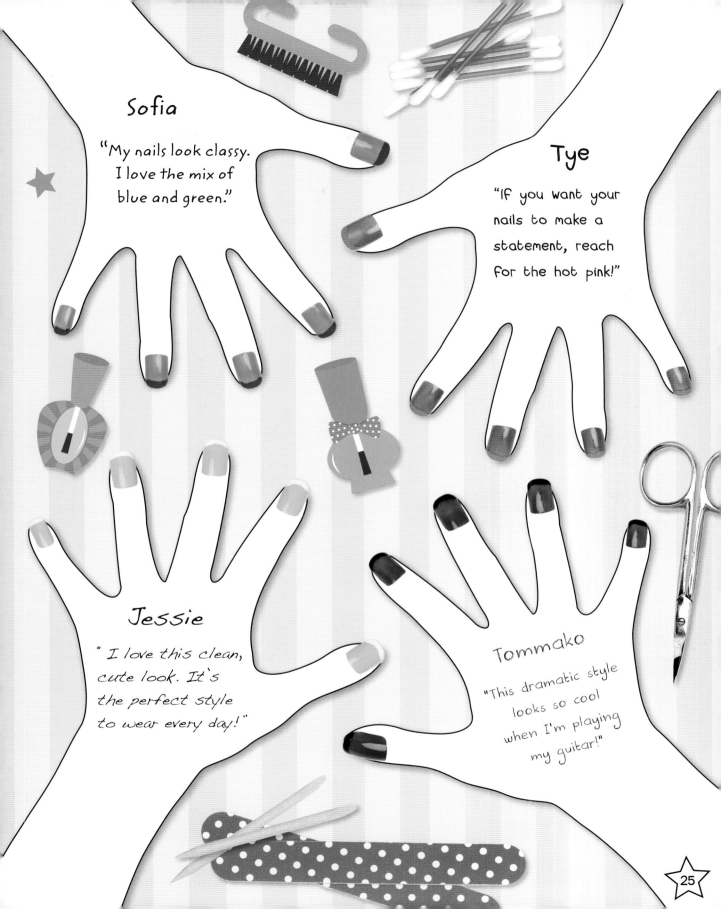

Sofia

"My nails look classy. I love the mix of blue and green."

Tye

"If you want your nails to make a statement, reach for the hot pink!"

Jessie

"I love this clean, cute look. It's the perfect style to wear every day!"

Tommako

"This dramatic style looks so cool when I'm playing my guitar!"

Art at Your Fingertips

There are so many things you can do with your nails. Find out how to make a masterpiece out of your next manicure.

Nail Pens

These cool nail pens allow you to draw on your nails and nail polish. If you have a steady hand (or a friend with one!) you can draw almost anything.

Gems

These teeny sparklers give your nails that instant bling-factor. They can be tricky to stick on, but they're worth the effort.

Stickers

If you want the look, but not the hassle, you can cheat and buy ready pre-designed nails that just stick right over your own nails. Pop them on and cut them to fit your real nails.

Glitter

Glittery nail polish gives an instant hit of glamor. Choose darker shades so the glitter really stands out.

YOU WILL NEED:

- Red nail polish
- White nail polish
- Bobby Pin grip
- Toothpick or white nail art pen

Polka Dot Nails

1

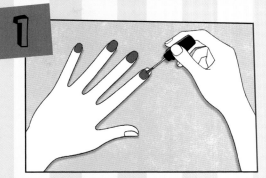

Paint your finger nails in a bright red shade. Do at least two coats and let it dry.

2

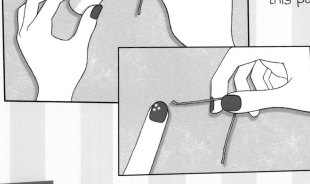
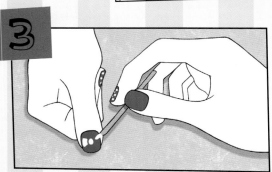

Take a bobby pin and straighten it out. Dip one end into some white nail polish and start to make your dots. Follow this pattern for perfect dots, but leave your thumbs blank.

3

On each thumb, use a toothpick dipped in the while nail polish (or a nail art pen if you have one) to draw a simple bow. Copy this design to help you.

Top Tip

To make your new nails last, use a clear nail polish or top coat on the top.

27

Hair Heaven

Want to feel fabulous from head to toe? Don't forget your hair! Try out these cool 'dos on your friends and yourself.

Know Your Face Shape

Look at your face shape in the mirror, then see which of these four pictures matches you best. Discover a style to suit you.

Heart

★ Long hair:
Try scooping it up into a neat, high ponytail on top of your head.

★ Short hair:
Add detail with cute clips to keep stray hairs off your face.

★ Afro hair:
Divide your hair into two low bunches that sit on, or just above, your shoulders.

★ Long hair:
Dry your hair roughly with a hairdryer, then add some texture with a little hairspray. Let the hair fall around your face for a messed up hippy style.

★ Short hair:
Side parts look really good with round face shapes. Keep your hair in place with clips.

★ Afro hair:
Leave your hair loose and natural. Wash and dry it as usual and just tease your curls with a comb.

Round

Square

★ Long hair:

Brush all your hair to one side and let it fall over your shoulder. Keep the back smooth with hair clips and hairspray.

★ Short hair:

If you usually tuck your hair behind your ears, let it fall forward for a change.

★ Afro hair:

Gather all your hair to one side and pin it in place with some pretty clips.

★ Long hair:

Brush your hair into a smooth, sleek center part and let it fall around your face.

★ Short hair:

Keep it neat! Smooth, sharp styles are perfect for oval face shapes. Try blow drying your hair straight for a sharper finish.

★ Afro hair:

Go big! Use your favorite product to add volume to your hair and backcomb sections to add height.

Oval

Hair Care

Remember these important rules for keeping your hair in tip-top condition.

1 Brush your hair every morning and before you go to bed to stop tangles from breaking your hair.

2 Maintain a healthy diet and drink plenty of water to keep your hair shiny.

3 Leave conditioner on your hair for at least three minutes before rinsing to give it time to work its magic.

Braid Brilliance

Braids look gorgeous whatever type of hair you have. See if you can master these two styles.

Top Tip
Try this style when your hair is slightly damp. When your hair dries, take out the braid to reveal wonderful wavy hair.

The French Braid

1 Take a section of hair from the top of your head, at the front of your hair line, and brush it through. Divide that section into three.

2 Begin to braid this section of hair by crossing each side section over into the middle. Start to gather up small pieces of hair from the rest of your head with each side section you cross over.

3 Keep gathering hair as you braid until all your hair is contained within the braid. You should end up with a pretty, neat style.

6

The Fishtail

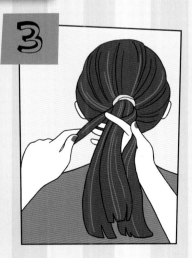

1 Put your hair in a ponytail and divide it into two equal sections.

2 Take a small piece of hair from the far side of one of your sections and add it to the inside of the other section.

3 Now take a small piece of hair from the far side of the other section, and add that piece to the inside of the first section.

4 ····▶ **6** Repeat until you run out of hair, then secure with a hair tie.

Book Night

Plan a book-filled night in and you're guaranteed to have a fabulous time!

It can be hard to find a book that all your friends have read, so ask your guests to bring their favorite book instead.

It could be:
- Their favorite bedtime book from when they were little
- A book about their favorite band or actor
- A novel
- A book full of yummy recipes.

Any book will do!

Make copies of this invitation then secretly slip them into the pages of your friends' books, ready to be discovered.

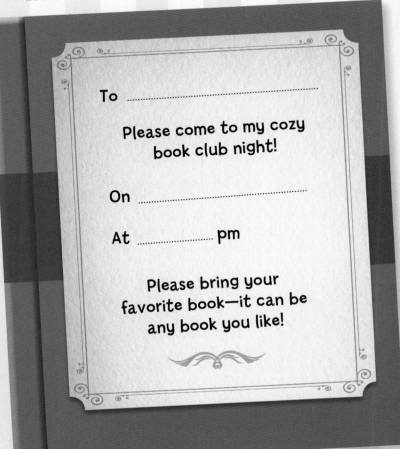

To ....

Please come to my cozy book club night!

On ....

At .... pm

Please bring your favorite book—it can be any book you like!

Literary Stars

Which book character are you most like? Answer the questions, then add up how many of each symbol you get.

1 You can buy one book from a book store. What do you choose?

☆ A novel you're going to read at school next semester.

■ Something by Jane Austen or Charles Dickens.

△ A book of ghost stories.

◯ A pretty notebook or journal.

2 Where's your favorite place to hang out with friends?

☆ At school between classes.

◯ Anywhere, as long as you're all together.

△ The park.

■ At home.

3 If one of your friends is upset, what do you do?

◯ Give her a big hug, then talk to a teacher or parent to work it out.

☆ Talk her through everything that's made her feel sad.

△ Go and talk to the person who's made her upset.

■ Come up with a way to make her feel better.

4 What do you most look forward to on a school day?

☆ Learning new things.

■ Chilling out in the library.

◯ Playing sports.

△ Seeing your friends at break.

5 What's your dream holiday destination?

△ Somewhere I've never been before.

☆ I'd prefer a "staycation."

■ Somewhere chill where I can read all day long.

◯ Camping in the countryside with family and friends.

6 What type of book would you love to write?

■ Just one type of book? I want to write many!

△ A vegetarian recipe book.

◯ A travel guide.

☆ A book all about my favorite subject.

Mostly ☆—Hermione

Just like Hermione from the *Harry Potter* books, you always know the right thing to do. You're super smart and love learning new things. Your friends love how you're always there if they need a helping hand.

Mostly ■—Matilda

You are really thoughtful and kind, and just like Roald Dahl's *Matilda*—you LOVE books! You can be a little shy, but that doesn't mean you're a pushover. You like to think things through and take your time over important decisions.

Mostly △—Bella

You love anything spooky, and there isn't much that scares you—just like Bella Swan from the vampire series *Twilight*. If there's an adventure, you'll be there! You have a close set of friends and would do anything to protect them.

Mostly ◯—Arwen

Arwen is a feisty Elf from *Lord of the Rings* who, like you, is great at making friends no matter who they are. You're friendly, caring, and talkative—and you look great no matter what you wear.

Write Your Own Book

Want to be the next J K Rowling? If you have an idea in your head,
try out these fun tips, then get writing.

 ## The Idea Bubble

So, you have a great idea, but you don't know where to take it next? Try creating an idea bubble to get your imagination buzzing. Write your idea in the middle of a piece of paper and draw a bubble around it, like this:

The three wishes

Now, draw lines coming off your bubble and write down anything that comes to mind.

What are they?

How?

The three wishes

Where does it happen?

Who gets them?

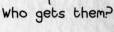

What are they?

Good or bad?

What happens?

Starts bad, ends good.

How?

The three wishes

Where does it happen?

Who gets them?

Short story or book?

At school

Keep drawing lines off your ideas until you've answered the questions and filled the page. That's the start of your story.

Timeline

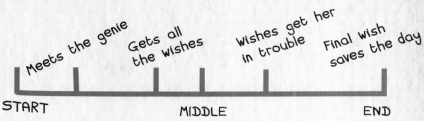

Meets the genie | Gets all the wishes | Wishes get her in trouble | Final wish saves the day

START   MIDDLE   END

You could draw the events on a timeline, like the one above.

Most stories follow a similar pattern:
Introduction, Action, Problem, Resolution.
You could plan out your story like this:

Introduction: Meeting the main characters—
Annie and the genie.
Action: Girl is granted three wishes.
Problem: Wishes get the girl into trouble.
Resolution: Girl uses last wish to fix everything.

Who's Who?

Your characters are really important, so it's worth taking the time to get to know them. Write down the names of each of your characters and make a little fact file about them. Keep these fact files with you as you write for inspiration— and so you don't forget anything important.

Name: Annie Walker
Age: 14
Lives: Kansas
Birthday: 4th May
Likes: Her dog, her best friends, drama
Dislikes: Terri Brown (the school bully), Math homework

Name: Jenny Genie
Age: 712
Lives: In a lamp
Birthday: She's forgotten!
Likes: Granting wishes, eating Turkish delight
Dislikes: Being stuck in her lamp, granting wishes that get people in trouble

Scribble or Tap It Out

The author Jacqueline Wilson writes all her novels in pretty notebooks before typing them out, but many authors like to go straight to their laptops. Why not try both and see which works best for you? Remember to save your work as you go and keep any notebooks safe.

Guess that Book

Challenge your friends to guess the book title without using any words!

What to Do:

1 Give each of your friends a sheet of paper and place your craft materials in the middle of a table so everyone can reach them.

2 Ask your friends to think of a book title (one that you will all know). Then get them to design a book cover without using any words.

3 When everyone has finished, line up the book covers and guess what each one is meant to be.

Can you guess what these books are?

1

2

3

36

The Neverending Story

Get your friends together to write the funniest story you've ever heard!

 Write the following on separate pieces of paper, then fold them up and put them in a bowl.

① It was a dark and stormy night when...

② (name) and (name) had had enough. So they decided to...

③ All of a sudden...

④ No one could believe it when (name of a celebrity) arrived! They...

⑤ Finally, it was time to go home, so everyone...

2 Ask each guest to pick out a piece of paper and finish off the sentences without telling anyone else what they are writing.

3 Starting with number one, each guest reads out what's written on their paper (or one guest can read everything in order).

Top Tip

Write out the funniest stories for your guests to take home!

You can play this game many times, so each guest has a turn at writing something different.

Secret Diary

Keeping a diary full of all your special thoughts and secrets is a lot of fun. Be sure to decorate it just the way you like.

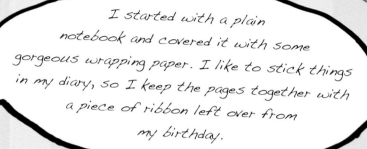

I started with a plain notebook and covered it with some gorgeous wrapping paper. I like to stick things in my diary, so I keep the pages together with a piece of ribbon left over from my birthday.

My diary is full of all the things I love, from fashion to friends. I cut out many pictures from magazines, as well as photos of my friends, and layer them up on the cover of my diary. I add more pics when I see ones I like.

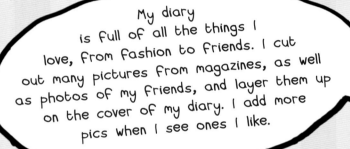

I keep all the tickets from places I have been (music concerts, the movies, even a train ride) and stick them on my diary. It's a great way to remember all the fun times I've had with my friends and family.

I change the cover of my diary all the time (that way no one realizes what it is!). I take a poster and wrap it around the cover of my diary. Then, when I get bored, I choose another one.

Crack the Code

If you want to keep something super secret in your diary, why not write a few words in code? There are many to try out.

1 **Front to back** – Simply move the first letter to the end of the word. So "diary" becomes "iaryd". Work it out: ym iaryd si ecrets!

2 **Backwards alphabet** – Each letter becomes something new! Here's a code cracker to help you:

A B C D E F G H I J K L M N O P Q R S T U V W X Y Z
Z Y X W V U T S R Q P O N M L K J I H G F E D C B A

Work it out: Gsrh rh girxpb!

3 **Mirror, mirror** – Write the words you want to be in code on a piece of paper, then look at it in the mirror and copy what you see into your diary. Simple!

Work it out (you can use a mirror to help):

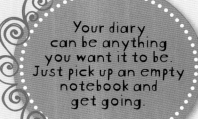

ƎMOƨƎWD ƎЯD ƨbnɘiЯꟻ ʎM

Your diary can be anything you want it to be. Just pick up an empty notebook and get going.

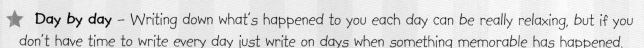

Get Writing!

Choose one, or all, of these to get your diary started.

⭐ **Day by day** – Writing down what's happened to you each day can be really relaxing, but if you don't have time to write every day just write on days when something memorable has happened.

⭐ **Dates** – You can keep your diary totally functional if you like. Write down your friends' and family's birthdays, homework dates, and fun trips so you know exactly what's coming up.

⭐ **Thoughts** – Sometimes an idea or a question will pop into your head out of the blue—that's when a diary can be really useful. Jot down cool dreams you've had, ideas, names of bands you hear on the radio, questions to research, and anything else that crosses your mind.

⭐ **The future** – It's great to visualize your hopes and dreams. It could be something you want in 10 years, or 10 days, but writing it down can make it feel more achievable.

Music Night

Whatever music you're into, sharing your favorite tunes with your friends and having a dance party can be so much fun.

Hit It!
Make sure your music night hits all the right notes with these top tips!

Set up a DJ area where your friends can bring their CDs and plug in their MP3 players.

Make sure each of your guests has a turn playing their favorite music.

Agree on a time to turn the music off—you can always carry on the fun with a silent dance-off

Grab a notebook to write down the names of any new songs and bands you like.

You are invited to rock out with

....

At the coolest new music venue in town. My house!

On .... At .... pm

Please bring your favorite tunes with you.
Dress code: comfy—and don't forget your dancing shoes!

Make a Date
Invite all your music-crazed friends to your night in with these super-cool invitations. Try writing in a silver pen!

I'm with the band!

Want to make a band with your friends?
Take this quiz to see what you should play!

YES →
NO →

START

Like to take the lead?

Drama is the BEST subject!

Got great rhythm?

Ever written a song?

Lyrics are more important than the tune!

Can you read music?

Music is your life!

Bags of energy?

Love to rock out?

Got to play it loud?

Singer
Like Tye, you just love being center stage. It's your job to tell the story of each song through the lyrics. Start memorizing the lyrics to your favorite tune right now.

Drummer
You love music, but you're more interested in having fun than working out melodies. Just like Sofia, you'll love being part of a band and can't wait to get playing.

Keyboards
Keyboard and piano players tend to be a bit shyer than the rest of the group. It's up to you to drive the tune of the song, so you're probably super-musical, just like Jessie.

Guitarist
Guitar players are the heart and soul of a band. Like Tommako, they adore music and take it very seriously. They LOVE to rock out!

Start a Band

Did you know that the members of most of the biggest bands in the world are also best friends? Why not find out if you and your friends can rock out, then turn your night in into the start of the coolest band ever!

Play on

The first thing to do is see how musical your friends are. If you already play an instrument, great! If none of you play any instruments, why not be a vocal group instead?

Practice Makes Perfect

Once you have your band together, come up with a time each week when you can meet up to rehearse. You could even follow your band rehearsals with a chill out session afterwards.

Top Tip

Most bands start off by trying to copy the songs of bands they love. That way they get used to playing together and can see who's best at what. Choose a favorite song you all know well and get started.

Band Name Generator!

So, now you have your band together, how about a name? Use the guide below to come up with an awesome name.

★ Whose birthday is next? What letter does her name begin with? That's the first part of your band name!

A–F: Sparkling
G–K: Little
L–Q: Amazing
R–U: Shimmering
V–Z: Superstar

★ Who has the longest name? What letter does her name begin with? That's the second part of your band name!

A–F: Wonders
G–K: Starlights
L–Q: Songsters
R–U: Diamonds
V–Z: Angels

We're the Little Diamonds!

Little Diamonds

Top Tip

Think of a subject you'd like your song to be about. It could be something that's happened to you, or it could just be a song all about you and your friends.

Make an Album Cover

Now you've got a super-cool name for your band,
why not design your first ever album cover?!

The Logo

Your logo says a lot about what kind of band you are, so you have to get it right. Take turns sketching out your band name—then vote to see which one you all like best, or mix them all together to create the ultimate logo.

All About You

The most important element of your cover is... you! Arrange yourselves in a cool pose and ask a grown-up to take a photo of you to put on the front. For a different look, you could cut out existing photos of yourselves and arrange them on the cover like a collage, or even draw a picture of you and your friends.

The Title

What's your first hit album going to be called?
Try this fun exercise to come up with a totally cool title.

1. Give each band member a piece of paper and a pen.

2. Ask them to write down the first three words that come to their mind when they think of your group.

3. Take turns reading out your list, and make a note of the words that appear more than once. The words that appear the most make up your album title!

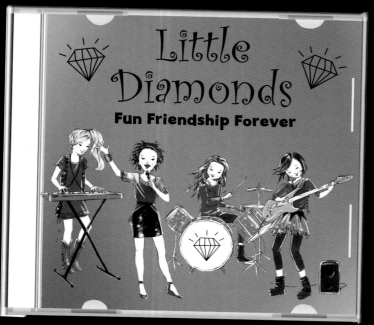

Top Tip

Finally, decorate your album however you like. You can keep it super-plain and all one color, or you can go crazy and stick on many things that represent you, like candy wrappers or ticket stubs.

Dance Party

Get your friends together for a musicfest, then choose your favorite tune to create a cool dance routine to.

Listen!

The first step to coming up with any routine is to listen to the song, many times. That way you'll get to know when there's a change in beat or where any slow parts crop up.

Plan!

Start coming up with moves for certain parts of the song, then write them down. The more you listen to the song, the more moves you'll start to think of.

Dance!

Now comes the fun part! Start the song and do the moves you have thought of. Don't be afraid to stop the song and go back to the beginning to make sure each section is perfect.

Here are some last minute tips before you perform...

★ Decide how you're going to stand together—it could be in a line or a diamond shape. You can switch it around as you dance.

★ When it comes to your dancing outfit, keep it comfy. Choose something you can move around in.

★ Keep a supply of drinks close by (water is perfect) to keep you hydrated while you dance.

Time to Perform

Now that you've come up with the best routine on the planet, you need to show off your moves. Why not perform in front of your family, or see if you can do it as part of a school show.

Fun Times

Playing games with your best friends can be so much fun! Use your next girl's night in to play some cool indoor games, and plan your next sporty day out, too.

Before your guests arrive, decide where you are going to hold your night in. It's probably best to choose a room that has a space for you all to sit around together comfortably. Wherever you decide to hold your party, clear away anything that could get knocked over in all the excitement.

Come and Play

Copy these fun invitations to give out to your friends. Remember to include all the essential info.

Top Tip

If you love board games, why not ask each of your guests to bring their favorite game with them so you can hold a board game marathon.

Get ready to have fun...

You are invited to the ultimate **games night!**

Taking place at ....

On ....

From ....pm

Get ready to play some awesome games!
Dress code: comfy.

How Competitive Are You?

Do you HAVE to win, or are you happy just playing? Read the questions and add up your scores to find out your gaming personality!

1 **It's time to pick teams! What are you thinking?**
a. Who's going to help me win?
b. Which team looks the strongest?
c. Where's my best friend?
d. Where could I help out most?

2 **Your favorite type of game is...**
a. Something that takes skill and determination.
b. A sports team game.
c. Something silly where we can all have fun.
d. A team board game.

3 **How do you feel when you lose a game?**
a. Lose? Sorry, I don't know the meaning of the word.
b. You're secretly really fed up, but you don't let on.
c. Absolutely fine! You might win next time.
d. Really happy for the winning team.

4 **What's your role when you play in a team?**
a. I'm the captain, of course!
b. I help out the person in charge and give them all my good ideas.
c. I'm just a member of the squad. I'm happy to do whatever I'm told.
d. I like to support the other players as much as I can.

5 **Which one of these would you love to win?**
a. A gold medal at the Olympic Games.
b. An Oscar.
c. A silly quiz show with your friends.
d. A charity marathon.

6 **Where do you see yourself in 10 years?**
a. Probably the head of a company—or super famous!
b. I'll be running my own small business.
c. Hopefully doing something I love with good friends around me.
d. Doing something worthwhile.

Now, add up your scores: A = 4   B = 3   C = 2   D = 1

21-24
Winner Takes It All!
Just like Tommako, you love to win! Otherwise, what's the point in playing the game? You enjoy working really hard. Just try to remember to have fun at the same time.

17-20
Cool Customer
Shhh! You actually LOVE winning, but you try to act like it doesn't matter. You'll play it cool and pretend you're just having fun, but all the time you're planning your next move.

11-16
Game Girl
You really enjoy playing games, but mostly because you get to have a giggle with your friends. You'd be just as happy watching a DVD or baking cupcakes, as long as you can spend time together.

6-10
Playful Pal
The main aspect of playing is taking part. You'd rather lose and let someone else win if it makes them happy, than see one of your friends upset. You play games to be creative or stay fit.

47

Be Awesome and Active

My friends and I love spending time together, having fun and staying fit. Read on to discover cool tips and amazing game ideas.

Being active is a great way to be healthy, but it's not just about getting up and moving around. Follow our top tips for a healthy lifestyle.

Keep Hydrated

Drink plenty of water; you need about seven glasses a day. It sounds like a lot, so keep a bottle of water with you wherever you go and just take sips when you're feeling thirsty.

Eat Well

When you're hungry, it can be really tempting just to grab a bag of chips—but it won't make you feel good for long! Try swapping chips for a crunchy apple or some raisins if you feel hungry between meals. Always try and eat five different types of fruit or vegetables in a day.

Sleep Time

Getting a good amount of sleep can help you be fit and healthy—around 10 hours is ideal. Going to bed at the same time each night keeps your body in a good routine so you have plenty of energy in the morning.

Super Sports

The next time you and your friends want to play a game outside, try one of these fun sports.

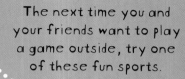

Tennis

Perfect for: Two or four friends who want to have fun.

You get fit by: Running, stretching, and using your arms to swing the racket.

What else: You don't need a tennis court to get going. Start by hitting a tennis ball to each other in your back yard or a park to practice your aim.

Soccer

Perfect for: Playing with a big group of friends.

You get fit by: Running around!

What else: Soccer helps your coordination as you have to run and kick the ball at the same time.

Running

Perfect for: Getting fit with friends or going solo.

You get fit by: Using lots of muscles and improving your breathing.

What else: The better you get, the faster and further you'll be able to run. Maybe one day you could run a marathon!

Basketball

Perfect for: Playing as a team.

You get fit by: Using your arms to dribble and throw the ball, and running around the court.

What else: You'll develop great hand-eye coordination as you try to dunk the ball through the hoop.

When it's raining or dark outside, why not play an indoor game?

★ Treasure Hunt!

Before your guests arrive, collect some random items from around your house—a rubber duck, paintbrush, and bright-colored T-shirt are all good ideas. Now, hide them around the room in which you are playing and give clues to your friends to find each one. You could split your friends into teams to make it even more of a challenge.

Paper and Pencil Games

Forget expensive game consoles or complicated board games; all you really need to have fun is a pencil and a piece of paper!

What am I Thinking?

1 Think of the name of a *book*, movie or TV show and write down dashes for the number of letters in the name.

2 Ask your friends to take turns calling out letters. If the letter is in the name of your TV show, movie or *book*, write it in—if it's not, the caller is out of the round.

3 Each friend gets to call out a letter and make a guess on their turn.

Squares

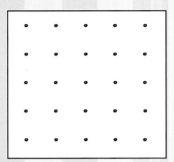

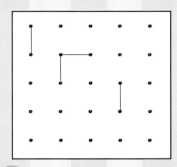

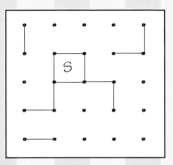

1 First, draw a grid of dots on a piece of paper, like this.

2 Next, take turns drawing lines between two dots.

3 If the line you draw makes a square, write your initial inside it. The person who makes the most squares is the winner!

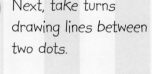

Ask the Oracle!

Find the answer to any question with this cool paper fortune teller.

1 Copy the design below onto a piece of paper.

2 Fold it in half, then in half again, and open it up so that the creases form a cross shape.

3 Flip the paper over; now fold each corner over so that the tip touches the middle of the paper.

4 Flip it over again and do the same on the other side.

5 Finally, slide your thumb and index finger into the flaps to create a square shape you can move.

How to Play:

1 Ask the oracle a fun question, then choose a color. Whoever is working the oracle must move it in and out while spelling out the color.

2 Then choose a number. The oracle is moved that number of times.

3 Finally, choose one more number. Look under the flap to receive your answer!

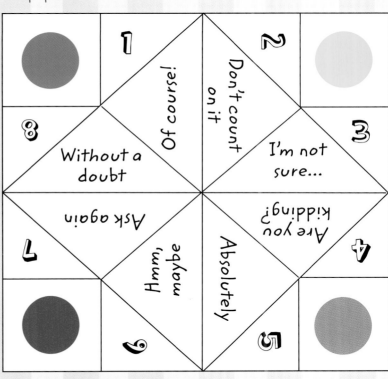

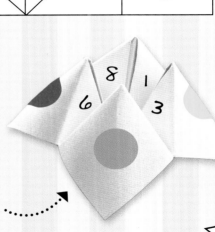

Your oracle should look like this.

Natural yogurt

Mixed berries

Fruit Smoothie

Banana

There's no denying it, smoothies are delicious! And you can make them out of pretty much any fruit you like. Learn how to make this simple smoothie, then get creative with your own flavor combos.

Mixed seeds

YOU WILL NEED:

- One banana
- Handful of strawberries
- 2 cups of yogurt
- Squeeze of lemon juice
- Knife
- Chopping board
- Spoon
- Fork
- Blender (if you have one) or a jug and a sifter

Peel and chop the banana, then take the hull out of the strawberries and chop the strawberries in half.

If you have a blender at home, put all the fruit, yogurt, and lemon juice inside and blend until it's smooth enough to drink. You may need to ask an adult to help you. If you don't have a blender, move on to step 3.

Mash the banana and strawberries with the back of a fork until they start to get gloopy. Put the fruit in a large jug with the yogurt and lemon juice and give it all a good stir. Finally, pour your smoothie into a cup through a sifter to catch any lumps.

Super smooth and ready to enjoy!

Blueberries are super healthy and yummy, too. I mix them with yogurt, a spoonful of honey, and some crushed ice. It turns a cool shade of purple!

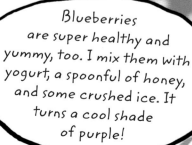

Fruity Granola Bars

Keep your energy levels high and your hunger pangs low with this tasty healthy snack.

YOU WILL NEED:

- 6 tbsp maple syrup
- 6 tbsp dried fruit (your choice!)
- 2 cups of unsalted butter
- 2.5 cups of quick-cooking oats
- Baking pan
- Baking paper
- Pan
- Wooden spoon

1

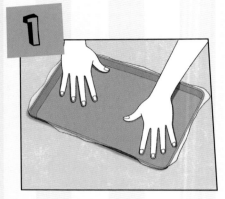

Preheat your oven to 350 F, then line a baking pan with baking paper.

2

Carefully stir the butter and syrup in a pan over a low heat until they have melted together.

3

In a large mixing bowl, stir the oats and dried fruit together. You can choose whatever fruit you like, but raisins and cranberries go well together.

4

Now carefully add the melted butter and syrup a little at a time, stirring until you get a big, sticky mixture.

5

Finally, spread your mixture onto your baking pan and cook for around 25 minutes (or until the top is slightly golden). Remove from the oven and leave to cool before cutting into squares to serve.

Oats

Raisins

Cranberries

It's a good idea to take a break from playing games and sit down to recharge. These light snacks are just right!

A glass of chilled milk goes perfectly with these chewy treats. Plus, milk is packed with vitamins and calcium, which are really good for you.

Dried fruit and oats are super energy boosters!

Fashion Night

Go through your wardrobe and flip through your favorite fashion magazines—your night in is going to be fashion fab-u-lous!

Let your friends know just what to expect from your fun fashion party with these trendy invitations. Copy or trace this design, then fill in all the important information.

Top Tip

Make sure any drinks and nibbles are kept away from your fashion wardrobes. It would be a disaster to make the perfect outfit, only to have it stained with orange juice or salsa!

You are invited to
My totally fashionable night in!
Taking place at

....

On ....

At .... **pm**

Please bring some clothes or accessories you no longer want, plus your fave magazines.

Dress Code: whatever makes you feel fabulous!

You're almost ready to start your fashion party. Get in the mood by finding out what your fashion focus is...

What's Your Fashion Focus?

Do this quiz before planning your next amazing outfit!

1 You spot a gorgeous top in a store window; what's the first thing you think about?
a. I have to have it before anyone else gets it.
b. Hmm, what do I have at home to go with it?
c. Perfect! I'll look around then get it if there's nothing else I like.
d. I wonder if I could find something similar in the thrift store around the corner?

2 There's something you want in a magazine, but it's expensive...What do you do?
a. Save up, or ask your parents for a loan.
b. Cut out the picture, then see what you already have in your wardrobe that you could upcycle.
c. Use it for inspiration on your next shopping trip and look for something cheaper.
d. Wait for it to go on sale.

3 Who's your fashion icon?
a. Someone famous with fabulous style.
b. Your big sister, or your mom when she was your age.
c. Your friends.
d. The lead singer of your fave band.

4 What are thrift stores for?
a. Offloading all your old clothes.
b. Selling cool clothes and raising money for good causes.
c. Finding interesting old books.
d. Finding one-of-a-kind totally awesome items.

5 What's your dream shopping day?
a. An unlimited supply of money and a huge mall.
b. Many independent stores and vintage stalls.
c. Anything, as long as I am hanging out with my friends.
d. Everything I like in the same place.

6 What colors do you love to wear?
a. Bright, interesting shades like turquoise.
b. Soft pastels—especially pink.
c. Mellow yellow.
d. Black, red, and purple.

Mostly "a"s - So Trendy
For you, fashion is about being up to date with all the latest styles. If your fave actress was snapped wearing it, then it's OK by you. Like Tye, you love clothes that make you feel confident and get you compliments wherever you go.

Mostly "b"s - Clothes with Heart
Whether it's organic cotton or recycled from a thrift store, you and Jessie like your clothes to tell a story. It's even better if your clothes are one of a kind, so you love turning unwanted items into cool, new fashion statements.

Mostly "c"s - Matching Moods
You like your clothes to work for you, not the other way around. If you're feeling sporty, you'll grab your sweats and a hat - if you fancy a duvet day, it's all about the onesie! You don't mind if your clothes aren't the latest trends because, just like Sofia, you are relaxed about your style.

Mostly "d"s - Fashion Drama
Just like Tommako, you like your clothes to reflect your personality—in a big way. You love anything that makes people sit up and take notice. Bright red leggings paired with a black tutu? Just your average Wednesday...!

Get Swishing!

Swishing is when you swap clothes you no longer want with your friends. It's an awesome way to clear out your wardrobe and create a whole new outfit for free.

Setting Up

Before your guests arrive, divide your room into sections for tops, bottoms, dresses, and accessories. When everyone turns up with their clothes, ask them to put their items in the right place. Don't forget to set up an area for trying things on.

What to Give Away

Decluttering your wardrobe can be tricky. Put all your clothes on your bed or floor and look at each item. If you haven't worn it in a year, it probably means you're not going to wear it again. Get rid of anything that doesn't fit you—it might fit one of your friends perfectly.

The Rules

1) Once all the items have been laid out, everyone gets to take a look at what's available. Give your friends a pen and piece of paper to write down what they like.

2) When everyone has had a good rummage, take turns saying what you would like. If no one else wants it—it's yours. If more than one of you wants the same item, move on to rule three...

3) When two or more people want the same thing you can either work it out between you, or flip a coin to decide who gets it.

4) Once everyone has bagged their favorite items, gather up whatever is left and put it into bags. Drop them off at a thrift store or donate to a local yard sale.

> I want to try something with a bit more of a rock-chick style, like Tommako.

> My style isn't that girly so I want to try out this pretty dress from Tye.

What to Look Out for

Pretend your swishing party is your favorite store. If something catches your eye, think: "Would I buy this?". Try not to pick things you "sort-of" like just because they're free, or you'll end up bringing home more things than you came with!

Turn to page 65 to find out how to use your new clothes in a cool fashion show!

Style the Seasons

Be stylish all year-round with our cool fashion planner.

Spring
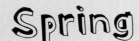

Spring is all about layers. One moment you could be strolling in a warm breeze, then there might be a thunderstorm. Think light, bright colors to cheer you up after winter and get you ready for summer.

Jessie's Spring Essentials!

Raincoat – You never know!

Floaty cardigan – Throw it over a cute top to keep you warm.

Ballet flats – It's not quite time for flip-flops.

Jeans – Ready for any weather.

Summer

I love summer! Going on picnics and having fun in the sun is so great, and it's my favorite fashion season, too. Get out your prettiest summer dresses, skirts, and shorts.

Sofia's Summer Essentials!

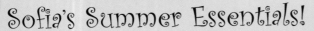

Sun hat – Keep cool and look cool, too.

Sunglasses – Squinting is so last season.

Maxi skirt – Pair it with a vest or floaty top.

Sandals – Pick a comfy pair you can wear with skirts and pants.

Fall

I love bundling up when it starts to get colder outdoors. Choose dark greens, blues, and reds and dig out your favorite scarf. Fall is the BEST season for showing off your new wardrobe on long walks in the park.

Tommako's Fall Essentials!

Boots – Choose a pair that will see you through the winter.

Tights – Wear lots of different colors to brighten up a dark outfit.

Beanie hat – Looks cool and keeps your head warm, too.

Jumper dress – Pair it with your tights and boots.

Winter

Ok, so it might be cold outside, but that doesn't mean your wardrobe can't be hot. I love winter, there are many parties to go to and everything has an added sparkle.

Tye's Winter Essentials!

Gloves, hat, and scarf – Take them with you wherever you go to stop the chills from getting in.

Cute coat – Your coat will be the one item in your wardrobe you wear every day, so make it a good one.

Leggings – Wear them instead of tights to keep you extra warm.

Party dress – The MOST important winter item!

TOP TIP
Store your out of season clothes away when you're not using them to create room in your wardrobe.

Be a Designer

Have you ever wandered around the stores looking for that perfect outfit? Why not design it yourself instead?

Mood Board

Create a pinboard full of ideas and things you love. It could include pictures from magazines, swatches of fabric, doll's clothes—anything goes! You could even create an online scrapbook (try www.pinterest.com to get you started). Once your board is full, you can pick out the best pieces to put in your design.

Mix and Match

Once you're done with a magazine, don't put it straight in the recycling bin. Keep a pile ready for design inspiration. Flip through and cut out any clothes that catch your eye. Put them into piles of tops, skirts, bottoms, dresses, and shoes.

When you have a good stack, it's time to start creating outfits. Mix and match different items to see what works well. Use a glue stick to stick the pieces down and pin your outfit to your mood board.

Make a Collection

When fashion designers are preparing for a big fashion show, they create a "collection". This just means many different outfits that have the same theme. It could be a certain color or type of fabric. Pick out what you like best about your first outfit and use that to start your next one. Soon you'll have a whole collection full of amazing designs.

How to draw your own designs

① Start with a really basic outline. You can trace one from a picture if you find it tricky to draw freehand.

② Draw over the outline with a black pen to make it stand out. Next, put a piece of paper over the top so you can see your outline underneath. Start sketching your clothes.

③ Start with simple things like T-shirts, skirts, and jeans. Once you have the basic style, you can start adding more detail and your designs can really take shape.

④ When you have finished your sketch, color it in. Keep your favorite designs in a special book (this is called a "Look Book" in the fashion world).

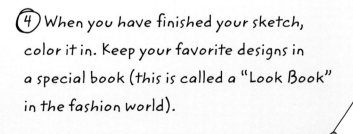

Catwalk Queens

So, now you know the coolest fashion tips around, are you ready to strut your stuff on the catwalk?

Get Styling

Before you take to the runway, you'll need to look your best. Pair up and decide which one of you will be the stylist and which one will be the model (don't worry, you can swap around later on).

The Clothes

As the stylist, you'll first need to decide on an outfit. You could borrow clothes from friends, or even dive into the swishing pile. Remember to accessorize. Once you come up with a gorgeous outfit, ask your model to walk up and down the room so you can see how the clothes "move". Make any little tweaks you need before the big show.

When you've had a turn at being the stylist, swap roles so your friend can have a turn— it's now up to you to be the model.

On the Catwalk

Time to show off those new creations! Set up your catwalk, watch the models, and decide which outfit you like the best.

The catwalk:

Catwalks don't have to be on a raised stage, you can make one in your own living room. Create a long walkway in the middle of the room. Line it with chairs or cushions for your friends to sit on while they watch.

The music:

Play your favorite tracks for the models to walk and pose to. Upbeat songs work best.

The pose:

Each model gets a turn at walking down the catwalk. When they reach the end, they should strike their best model pose, then walk back again.

Line up:

When all the models have walked the catwalk, they should line up and *be* ready to have their outfits judged.

Top Tip

Create awards for the best outfit, the craziest outfit, the funniest outfit, and the best model, too!

Just For Crafts

I love making things, whether it's turning something old into a gorgeous item or making something from scratch. Get your friends together for a cool crafting session.

Can You "Make" It?

Hand these sweet, homemade invitations out to your friends to get them in the crafting mood!

You are invited to my cool and crafty girl's night in!

On ....

Taking place at

....

At .... **pm**

Please bring an apron or old clothes!

What's Your Craft Calling?

Are you a creative chef or a whizz with a pair of knitting needles? Find out in our fun quiz!

1 When it comes to crafts, you have a lot of patience.

• Not really! Go to question 2
• Yes! Go to question 3

2 Is following a pattern sensible or just sooo boring?

• It's a good idea. Go to question 4
• Yawn! Go to question 5

3 Do you love giving your crafty creations away to your friends?

• Yes! It's the main reason I do it. Go to question 6
• Sometimes, it depends if I like the end result. Go to question 4

4 Do you often spend days making something?

• Hmmm, I'd prefer an afternoon.
You're a Baking buddy!
• Yes, totally! You're a Knitting Nancy!

5 Are you good at using your hands?

• Sometimes... Go to question 6
• Totally. You're a Customizing Cutie!

6 Crafts are best when you can do them AND chat to your friends at the same time.

• RIGHT! And put your feet up and chill out.
You're a Knitting Nancy!
• Only if they don't distract me too much...
You're a Baking Buddy!
• No way, when I'm crafting I'm in the zone.
You've got Painting Power!

Customizing Cutie
You use your crafting skill to turn old clothes into fashion statements! Turning a pair of old jeans into a skirt is your idea of crafting heaven. Like Tye, you're probably great at using your hands and love learning new skills.

Baking Buddy
Yum! Baking for you and Jessie is super relaxing and makes you feel all fuzzy inside. If you're not a super baker just yet, start with something simple like cupcakes. The best part about baking is you get to share the results with your friends.

Painting Power
Tommako loves to paint because, just like you, she adores being artistic. It doesn't matter if what you end up with isn't quite what you planned—that's the great thing about painting, you can be super creative.

Knitting Nancy
Once you get the hang of it, you can knit anywhere! It's a great craft for sharing with your friends or getting done while watching TV. You'll need patience, though, as getting to the end result can take time.

67

Getting Started

The key to making your crafty girls' night in go as smoothly as possible is... preparation! No one wants to get to that crucial stage in a craft, only to discover they've run out of glue or thread. Read on to ensure your crafting table is up to scratch.

Read Up!

Once you've decided on a craft, find out exactly what you will need and make a list. Remember to think about how many friends are coming and make sure there are enough materials for all.

Table or Circle?

Friends can share a pair of scissors between two, but make sure there are enough craft materials for each guest.

Depending on the craft you choose, you might find it better to sit at a table, or on the floor in a circle. Crafts that use paint or glue are easier on a table covered with newspaper, whereas things like sewing and knitting are great for when you are all sitting together on some comfy cushions.

Thirsty Work

Your guests are bound to get hungry and thirsty while they are creating their masterpieces, but you don't want anything to ruin your crafts. Serve drinks in bottles with screw tops to avoid spills over your brand-new bunting! Choose snacks that aren't too messy or greasy—popcorn is perfect.

Take It Easy

Whatever you decide to do (baking, sewing, painting...) there will always be some friends who pick it up really quickly, and some who find it more difficult. Choose a craft that everyone can enjoy, no matter what their crafting skills are like. Making a friendship bracelet or cupcakes could be really simple, or very complicated.

Crafty Guidelines

- If it's messy—put down newspaper! Paint, glue, and glitter can all make a mess so it's best to cover any surfaces and ask your friends to wear an apron or old clothes.

- Keep it simple! Don't try to be too ambitious—especially on your first go.

- Recycle—try to use as many recyclable materials as possible, and if you have anything left over, put it back in the recycling bin.

- Have fun! As well as making something gorgeous, you want to make sure you have a good time. Don't worry if not everything goes according to plan.

Top Tip

If you have a friend who is great at a particular craft, why not ask them to "lead" the session? They can make their craft step-by-step for your friends to follow.

Friendship ♥ Bracelets

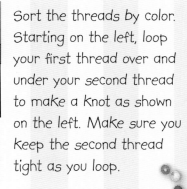

Get creative and show the world just how much your friends mean to you by making some gorgeous friendship bracelets!

YOU WILL NEED:

- Cotton thread in three colors
- Tape

1

Choose three colors for your bracelet. Take two threads of each color (about 12 inches long) and tie them together in a knot. Tape the knotted end to the edge of a table.

2

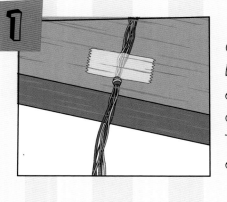

Sort the threads by color. Starting on the left, loop your first thread over and under your second thread to make a knot as shown on the left. Make sure you keep the second thread tight as you loop.

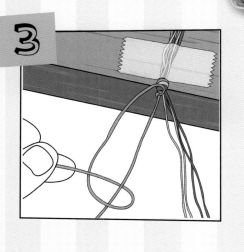

Pull the knot so it's nice and snug at the top of your bracelet, then repeat the step so you have a double knot.

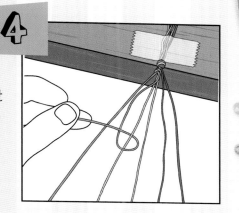

Move on to the next thread along the row and repeat steps 2 and 3, then continue until the first thread has made a double knot with each of the other threads.

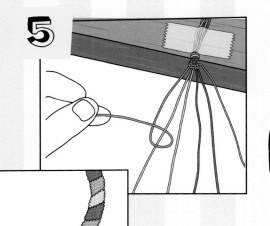

Remember to check that the bracelet fits and leave enough thread on either side to tie it on.

Now take the second thread (which will now be the one on the far left in your row of threads) and repeat the process. Continue the steps with each line of thread. Keep going until your friendship bracelet is long enough to go round your wrist. Tie all the threads in a knot when you're finished.

I love chunky bracelets in lots of wild colors. I'm going to make a lot more because I think they totally rock!

Tommako

Sofia

My bracelets show off my style, even when I'm playing tennis—they're super light and don't get in the way.

Why Not Try?

1 Create super-thin bracelets by using just three very long (1 yard) threads.

2 Tie them together in a knot at one end, pick one thread, and hold it out to the left.

3 Knot this thread around both of the other two threads. Keep going until you want to change color.

4 To do this, simply hold the new thread out to the left and knot it around the other two strands.

5 Once you've finished, don't forget to tie all the threads together in a knot. Perfect!

For something extra special why not try adding beads. It's best if you thread them along the strands that are being knotted.

Make bracelets for all of your friends.

Tye

Bracelets with one or two colors are super stylish. I try to match them with a part of my outfit, like my shoes or bag. So cool!

Jessie

Each bracelet means so much to me, as one of my amazing friends made it. They always make me smile when I look at them.

Fab Frames

Make these cute vintage-looking frames, then fill them with photos of your best friends.

1

⚠ Before you start, remove the glass and back of your frame and keep them somewhere safe. Measure the width of your frame shape.

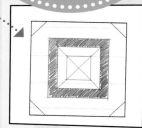

Place your frame on the back of your fabric and draw around it, inside and out. Remove the frame. Shade lightly on the material to show where the frame will go. Draw another square around this with a ruler, matching the width. Now draw a cross from each of the corners of the shaded square and draw a small square halfway between the start of the lines and where they cross.

2

In the outermost square draw a line across each of the corners. Carefully cut along the cross in the middle of your frame shape and cut out the small middle square. Snip off the outer corners, too.

3

Fold the material of the inner square back on itself, but not so it fully overlaps and glue it in place. This will stop the fabric from fraying.

4

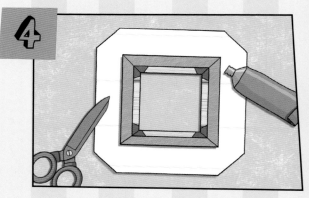

Place the frame back onto your fabric. Fold the inner square again, but this time so the material overlaps the inside of the frame. Glue the fabric to the frame.

5

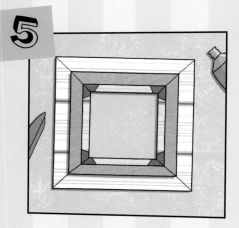

Now fold the outer square of your fabric back on itself and glue the fabric together.

Tie a bow with some pretty ribbon and glue it to the corner of your frame.

6

Start to fold one corner at a time. You'll need to fold twice to get a neat edge. This should overlap the corners of the frame. Glue the fabric to the frame.

Decorate the corners with mismatched buttons.

7

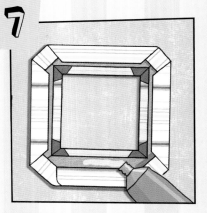

Now fold in each side of the outer square so that it overlaps the frame. Glue the fabric and frame together.

Pop the glass back in your frame, add a cool photo, and replace the back. Ta-da!

Adorable Hangers

Keep your favorite outfits in perfect condition with these luxury hangers. They'll brighten up your wardrobe, too!

YOU WILL NEED:

- Old clothes hanger (a wooden one with a single bar across is best)
- Stuffing
- Ruler
- Scissors
- Needle and thread
- Fabric
- Ribbon
- Iron

1

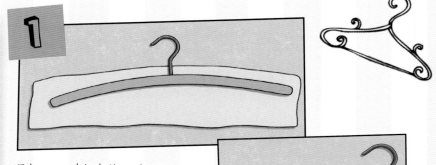

Take an old clothes hanger and wrap your stuffing around it. Secure it in place with long stitches. This doesn't have to be neat as it won't be seen.

2

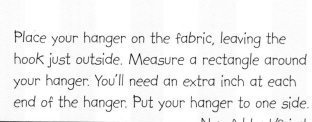

Place your hanger on the fabric, leaving the hook just outside. Measure a rectangle around your hanger. You'll need an extra inch at each end of the hanger. Put your hanger to one side.

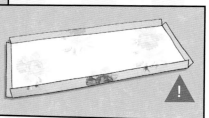

Now fold a 1/3 inch hem on all sides and flatten with a hot iron to keep it in place. Ask an adult to help.

3

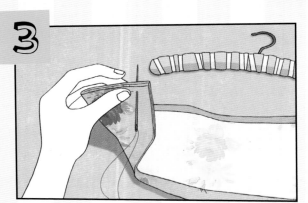

Fold your material in half, lengthways. Now sew up each end of your fabric. As you sew, try to bunch and gather your material so you start to make a sausage shape.

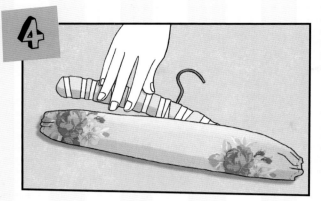

Carefully slip your hanger inside the tube of fabric.

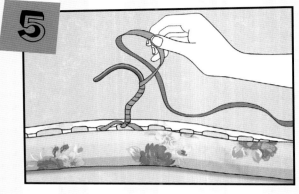

Take a long piece of ribbon (around 24 inches), and secure it with a stitch to the wadding at the base of the hook. Wind the ribbon tightly up and down the hook, finishing it with a stitch.

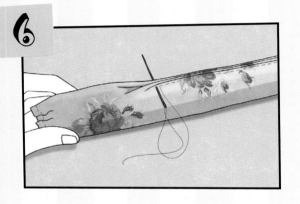

Now it's time to sew up the rest of your hanger. Pinch the two sides together and sew a running stitch along the hems. You can always pin it together first to make it a little easier.

Tie a pretty ribbon around the bottom of the hook in a bow.

Top Tip

Sprinkle some dried lavender into your hanger before sewing it up to give your wardrobe a nice fresh scent.

Make a Cozy Cushion

It's time to snuggle up with these gorgeous cushions. Make them for all of your friends.

1

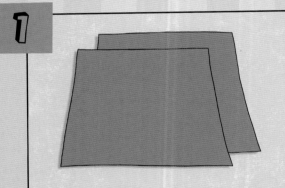

Place your cushion pad on your fleece fabric and measure a square that is 1 inch bigger on all sides. Cut out the square. Then cut out another square the same size from the same color.

2

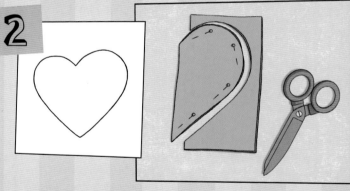

Draw a heart template (smaller than your cushion pieces) on a piece of paper and cut it out. Now take your different colored fleece fabric and cut out a square slightly bigger than the heart template. Fold the square of fabric in half and pin your heart template to it as shown. Then cut it out.

3

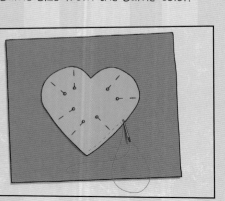

Place your fabric heart shape on one of the fleece squares and pin it in place. Sew the heart onto the square using a running stitch.

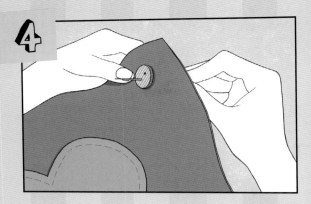

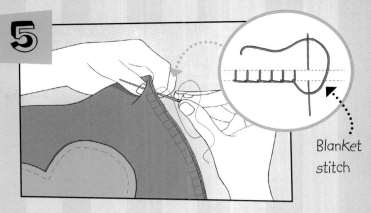

Blanket
stitch

On the same square as your heart, sew a button in each corner at least 2 inches in from the edge. If you have enough buttons you can sew one in the middle of your heart, too.

Now place the two squares together—make sure your heart is on the outside. A blanket stitch is the best way to sew them together, but if you find this tricky, use a running stitch instead.

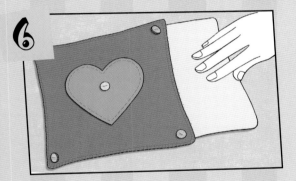

When you have sewn three sides, push the cushion pad inside. Pin the final side to keep it together as you sew.

Follow the same steps but use a star motif instead!

Brilliant Bunting

Give your room a pretty, vintage feel by making this simple bunting!

> You can use any fabric you like for this craft, from unwanted towels, table-cloths to old clothes!

1

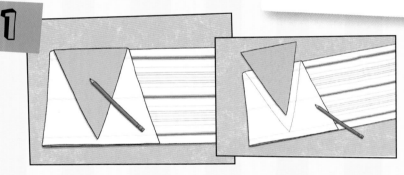

First, draw a tall triangle shape on a piece of paper and cut it out to make your template. Place the template on the back of some fabric and draw around it. You could even fold the fabric over to create two triangles at once.

2

Carefully cut out your triangles. Use pinking shears if you have them as this will stop the fabric from fraying. Once you have all your triangles cut out from the different fabrics, mix them up to create a pretty pattern.

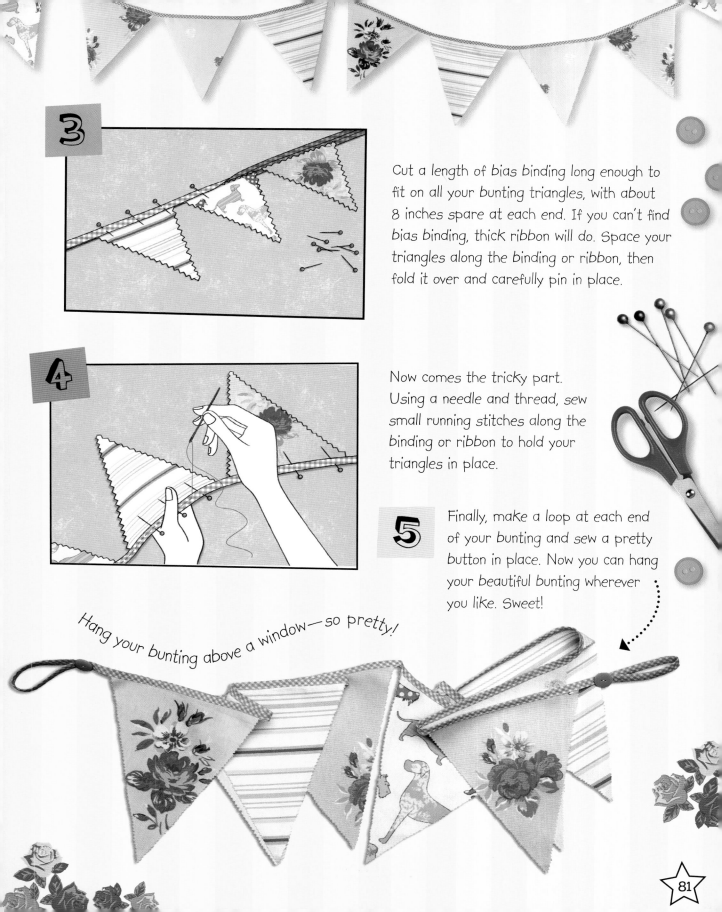

3 Cut a length of bias binding long enough to fit on all your bunting triangles, with about 8 inches spare at each end. If you can't find bias binding, thick ribbon will do. Space your triangles along the binding or ribbon, then fold it over and carefully pin in place.

4 Now comes the tricky part. Using a needle and thread, sew small running stitches along the binding or ribbon to hold your triangles in place.

5 Finally, make a loop at each end of your bunting and sew a pretty button in place. Now you can hang your *beautiful bunting* wherever you like. Sweet!

Hang your bunting above a window—so pretty!

Crafty Cards

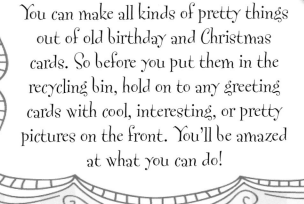

You can make all kinds of pretty things out of old birthday and Christmas cards. So before you put them in the recycling bin, hold on to any greeting cards with cool, interesting, or pretty pictures on the front. You'll be amazed at what you can do!

YOU WILL NEED:

- Colored stock card
- Old greeting cards
- Scissors
- Glue
- Ribbon
- Buttons
- Glitter
- Hole punch

Homemade Cards

Carefully cut out any pictures you like from your old greeting cards to create beautiful homemade new ones. Fold a letter-size piece of stock card in half to make your card shape. Then all you have to do is create your design. You could add ribbon, buttons, or glitter to make your cards extra special.

THANK YOU

Happy Birthday

Gift Tags

Use any leftover blank card from your greetings cards to make pretty tags. Simply cut out rectangle shapes and snip the corners at one end. Use a hole punch to make a hole for a piece of ribbon to be pushed through and decorate with *buttons, ribbon,* or *glitter.*

Match your gift tag design to the card you give.

Keep a box full of bits and pieces for your crafts. Old cards, bits of ribbon, and even wrapping paper could be used again to make pretty new cards and tags.

Trim the top and bottom of your card with ribbon for a classic look!

Mini-cards are perfect for saying thank you.

PARTY TIME!

YOU'RE A STAR

Cute Cupcakes

We have all the top-secret tips to make your cupcakes look as good as the ones in those trendy bakeries! Learn how to make a cute bow and perfect rose, then flip over to see the girls' favorite decorating tips.

BASIC RECIPE:

Makes 12 cupcakes
- 1/2 cup of self-raising flour
- 1/2 cup of caster sugar
- 1/2 cup of butter
- Two large eggs
- Half a tsp of vanilla extract
- Bowl
- Baking tray
- 12 cupcake liners

1. Preheat your oven to 400°F, then place your cupcake liners on a baking tray.
2. Cream the butter and sugar together. This means stirring hard until the mixture is pale and fluffy.
3. Add your eggs one at a time, then the vanilla extract. Sift in the flour and gently stir it all together.
4. Spoon your mixture into your liners until they are about 2/3 full. Bake for 15 to 20 minutes.
5. Once golden, place on a wire rack and leave to cool before frosting.

Cupcake Decorating

There are many pretty cutters and tools you can use for cake decorating. If you don't have everything below, you can cut out shapes using a plastic toothpick.

YOU WILL NEED:

- Ready to roll fondant
- Buttercream frosting
- Stencils
- Cutters
- Decorations: silver, white, and pink balls etc.

⭐ How to Make a Beautiful Bow

1

Using ready to roll fondant cut out two rectangle shapes as shown above.

2

Fold the ends of the large rectangle into the middle and use a little water as "glue" to keep them in place.

3

Pinch together to make your bow shape, and then wrap the smaller rectangle around the middle.

4

To finish off, cut some small strips of fondant with a triangle cut out of the bottom and add them to the middle of your bow to look like ribbon.

⭐ How to Make an Icing Rose

The bigger the circles, the bigger the rose!

1

Cut four circles 1/2 inch in diameter. Line them up in an overlapping row.

2

Use a drop of water or edible glue to hold them together.

3

Carefully start to roll up your row of circles from the top to the bottom.

4

When you finish rolling your rose will look something like this.

5

Gently tease out the top edges to make the petal shapes.

85

Cupcake Style

Now you've learned some cool techniques, check out the girls' designs. You can copy their ideas, or mix and match to find your own style.

Want to make a vintage-style cupcake? You could layer it up using different techniques.

1 Take a plain cupcake.

2 Add a swirl of buttercream frosting using a frosting nozzle if you have one.

3 Cut out a small circle, two hearts and a flower. Make a small bow using the technique from the previous page.

4 Now layer them up.

Roses look super sweet on a cupcake. Try making different sizes for a really cool effect.

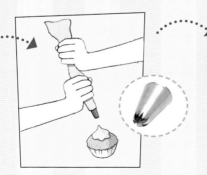

1 Take a plain cupcake.

2 Add a swirl of buttercream using a frosting nozzle if you have one.

3 Make one large rose and two smaller ones, using the technique from page 85, and then arrange them on the frosting.

Tiny patterns and polka dots look great on cupcakes! You might need a steady hand, but they look so cool when they are finished.

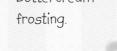

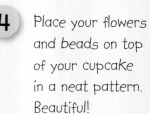

1 Take a plain cupcake.

2 Add a blob of buttercream frosting.

3 Cut a pink circle big enough to cover your cupcake from ready to roll fondant. Then cut out some small flower shapes. You'll need some edible silver balls and beads, too.

4 Place your flowers and beads on top of your cupcake in a neat pattern. Beautiful!

Why not use the bow as the star of your cupcakes? Add some small hearts for a nice finishing touch.

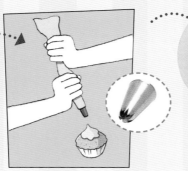

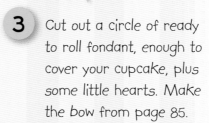

1 Take a plain cupcake.

2 Add a blob of buttercream frosting.

3 Cut out a circle of ready to roll fondant, enough to cover your cupcake, plus some little hearts. Make the bow from page 85.

4 Arrange your decorations. Use water or edible glue to hold them in place.

87

You Have Talent!

Putting on a talent show with your best friends is a fun way to spend a girls' night in. You might even discover a talent you never knew you had!

Copy this invitation and include an RSVP strip so your friends can say what they would like to do. Remember, not all of your friends will want to get up and perform—but there are other ways they can participate.

You Have Talent!

You are invited to take part in my talent show!

On ....

Taking place at ....

From .... pm

Please fill this in and hand it back to me. I can't wait to see you there!

☐ **YES!** I'd love to come to the talent show.
My talent will be ....

☐ **YES!** I'd love to come to the talent show, but I'd rather help out than perform.

☐ **Sorry,** I can't come. Have fun!

What's Your Secret Talent?

Are you always making up stories? Just can't stop singing?
Find out what your secret talent could be!

START

YES →
NO →

Love to perform?

Like making up stories?

Being fit is cool!

Spotlight on me? Cool!

Love to daydream?

Have to be the star?

Learning lines sounds easy.

Love spending time on your computer?

Love to move to music?

Dressing up is awesome!

Writer

You love being creative and losing yourself in your own world. Performing isn't your style. You're a super-supportive friend and a bit of a daydreamer. Who knows, you could be the next J K Rowling!

Dancer

You love music and can't stop your feet from moving when you hear it. Dancing is the perfect way to get active, have fun, and stay healthy. You like to get things right and your friends love how organized you are.

Singer

Whether it's in a musical or as the lead singer of a band, singing is your secret talent. You love to sing, hum, and whistle...it doesn't really matter as long as you are making music. You love being the center of attention.

Actress

You love performing, and being an actress is your dream job. Getting dressed up and being watched by all your friends sounds like your perfect night. You also love telling jokes and making your friends giggle.

Top Tips!

There are lots of things to think about before putting on your performance. Take a look at our top tips.

Take the Stage

A stage doesn't have to be on a platform or surrounded by chairs; it just needs to be a space big enough for your friends to perform on—and where the audience can see and hear them. If your night in is taking place in your living room, mark out a "performing area" with scarves or socks. Make sure everyone knows that this space is for performers only.

Running Order

As the host of the talent show, it's your job to work out who's going to perform and when. It's a good idea to mix up the types of talent on display—try not to put two singers next to each other, for example. If you have many performers with one type of talent, put everyone's name into a hat and pull out their names one by one to decide the order.

Feeling Nervous?

Even the most famous performers feel nervous before going on stage. Nerves just mean you are getting excited and a little bit scared. Most of the time nerves help you as they get you ready to go on stage, but if you don't like that jittery feeling here are some top tips on how to keep calm.

★ **Breathe!** It sounds silly, but sometimes when we get nervous we forget to breathe and this makes us feel lightheaded. Make sure you take big, deep breaths in through your nose and out through your mouth.

★ **Relax!** This trick is used by many stage actors before a big performance to make their bodies nice and loose. Lie on the floor and, starting with your toes, tense each part of your body for five seconds, then let it relax. Work your way up your body until you reach your head. When you get up, shake your arms and legs.

★ **Giggle!** Ask a friend who always makes you laugh to stay with you before you go on stage. Laughing releases lots of happy chemicals in our brains and eases tension.

★ **Go to the bathroom!** Stop smirking; this is actually a really good tip. If you go to the bathroom before your performance you'll feel much calmer. It will also distract you for a few moments before hitting the stage.

Behind the Scenes

Not all of your friends will want to put on a performance, so have a list of things for people to help out with so they feel part of the night.

Top Tip
Keeping the scoring secret will make sure no one's feelings get hurt.

★ **Judges!** Although your talent show is just for fun, having judges will give non-performers a fun job to do. Ask them to secretly score each performer out of 10, then add up the scores at the end to find an overall winner.

★ **Helpers** Ask each performer what they need for a performance and ask a helper to be their assistant. Helpers' jobs can include; assisting with costume and hair, starting the music on time, or handing the performer props.

★ **Audience warm up** Performing can be super scary, but if the audience start to clap and cheer as soon as you step on stage it's a big confidence boost. Ask non-performers to be as loud as possible when a performer comes on stage, and when they finish their show.

Top Secret
Judge's Comments

Read each statement below while watching the talent show. Give each performer a checkmark. You can add your own comments below the statements.

☐ 1. Amazing singing voice
....

☐ 2. Totally amazing talent
....

☐ 3. Lots of laughs
....

☐ 4. Awesome outfit
....

☐ 5. Dancing diva
....

☐ 6. Audience loves them!
....

Simply the Best!

The girls each have their own unique talents. Find out what award they would give to each other.

SOFIA
Chilled Chick

"I would give Sofia the Chilled Chick award, because she's always cool in a crisis. Nothing gets this girl down!"
– Tye

TYE
Designer of the Year

" Tye would definitely get the Designer of the Year award from me. She's always coming up with totally cool outfits and is the best at offering fashion advice." – Jessie

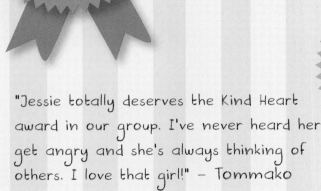

TOMMAKO
Music Genius

"The award I would give to Tommako would have to be Music Genius. She plays guitar AND piano, and her playlists are always amazing." – Sofia

JESSIE
Kind Heart

"Jessie totally deserves the Kind Heart award in our group. I've never heard her get angry and she's always thinking of others. I love that girl!" – Tommako

Get to the Top

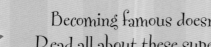

Becoming famous doesn't happen overnight (most of the time!).
Read all about these superstars to discover how they got to the top.

Name: J K Rowling

Profession: Author and creator of Harry Potter

Headlines: Sold over 450 million copies of her books—and still counting!

Her story: J K Rowling started writing when she was six years old. Every idea she had she would write down. She came up with the idea for Harry Potter while sitting on a train. At first, no one wanted to publish the book, but J K stayed strong and eventually it became a huge success.

What can I do? If you want to be a writer, the most important thing is to write! Keep a notebook and pen with you at all times for that moment when inspiration strikes. It's a good idea to read a lot, too, to get an idea of the styles you like. Ask your school if they have a writing club and if they don't—why not start one?

Name: Jessica Ennis-Hill

Profession: Track and field athlete

Headlines: Won gold at the 2012 London Olympic Games

Her story: Jessica has been training as an athlete since she was at school. She later joined an athletics club and was trained by the same coach who later took her to the Olympics. She took part in many competitions and trained every day.

What can I do? If you love sports, why not join a local sports club as well as a team at school? If you want to be as good as Jessica, you'll need to train hard—and that can mean before and after school. Try many different sports until you find the one you love.

Name: Taylor Swift

Profession: Singer-songwriter

Headlines: Taylor has won 7 Grammy Awards, 15 American Music Awards, 11 Country Music Association Awards, 7 Academy of Country Music Awards, 12 Billboard Music Awards, 17 BMI Awards, and many, many more... phew!

Her story: Taylor first sang in a musical theater group, before singing covers of her favorite songs. At 11 years old, after winning a talent competition, she decided that she wanted to write her own songs, so she learned to play the guitar. She pestered music companies until finally someone noticed her!

What can I do? Like Taylor, you can join a singing group or just start to record yourself singing your favorite songs. If you want to learn how to write songs, it's probably a good idea to take up an instrument first—guitar or piano would be perfect.

Name: Emma Watson

Profession: Actress

Headlines: Award-winning actress from the age of nine!

Her story: Emma knew she wanted to be an actress from the age of six and joined a theater club, which she went to after school. It was a teacher from the club who recommended her to play the part of Hermione in Harry Potter.

What can I do? Join a drama club. Many clubs take place after school or on weekends, so find one that suits you. If your school puts on plays see if you can get involved with them, too!

Becoming famous takes a lot of hard work, but also a bit of luck. If you find something you love, do it for the fun of it.

Index